Periplous

Periplous

The Twelve Voyages of Pytheas

Lesley Saunders

Shearsman Books

First published in the United Kingdom in 2016 by
Shearsman Books
50 Westons Hill Drive
Emersons Green
BRISTOL
BS16 7DF

Shearsman Books Ltd Registered Office
30–31 St. James Place, Mangotsfield, Bristol BS16 9JB
(this address not for correspondence)

www.shearsman.com

ISBN 978-1-84861-502-1

Copyright © Lesley Saunders, 2016

The right of Lesley Saunders to be identified as the author of this work has been asserted by her in accordance with the Copyrights, Designs and Patents Act of 1988. All rights reserved.

ACKNOWLEDGEMENTS

Thanks to David Morley for his encouragement of the idea; and to the editors of *The Warwick Review*, where an early extract of the poem was published.

A Greek merchant-explorer Pytheas – whose home port was the Greek colony of Massalia (Marseilles) – is said to be the first person to have circumnavigated the British Isles, in 325 BCE, thereby fixing the islands in the historical imagination as archipelagic, maritime, aloof. His own account of the voyage is lost.

I. Journey's jargon

Web-footed we've grown,
drifters with brackish beards
playing a hide-and-seek of peninsulas
with a minch of water. Once
I saw a woman washing
another woman's hair in a pail

but that was outside a tent
in a torn white night.
Hay-moon of midges, a wailing child.
Our sails are ripped and sodden,
we paddle around and around, Kantion
Belerion Orkas Belerion Orkas

Kantion, the blue tattoo
of ridge-pines on a too-far mountain,
the paint of their war-cries,
the lack of guest ethic, just the salt-
lick of our fingers no honey
a knuckle of bread no milk,

hallucinating again
a woman with dripping hair
Tethys in her drownedness kelp-like,
the psychogeography of rapefields
and scythe-wheeled clearings
our postcard home.

Offshore we sit at dark tables
of angles and tangents, our tell-tales
flap against the berg of sky.
This is the iron age,
too much subject to the Bear,
and we are waiting for what –

the Romans to come with their *pax* and leather umbrellas?

II. Armada

Flare. A blare of fire on the moor. And now
over there gilding the crest-feathers
of the inrushing tide a forest
of coals burning bright as a lucifer, a surf
of flame, a flagrancy, Helen once again
on the pyre of Troy *aglaos*

in the search-and-destroy arc-lights
in her petticoat her tiara
of scorched hair the hill-fort
of hot ash and the pretty god Siva
with bells on his toes spinning the length
of the fence from shore to shore

rousing the twelve fair counties
against the armada fall of the city
Carthage Massalia Graveney Marsh.
We were there. As the sun dropped
into the bay we stood to
and stared at the wave of fire

spreading steadily out through the night
from beachy head to the chalk horse, torching
the peak of the high peak, then the cheviots
and teviot, even as far as the slieves
and the treehouse on the savannah
et commixtam Volcanus ad astra favillam

till in the hour before dawn we saw
a paper boat come gliding downriver
with its small quivering flame, a mayfly alight
for less than a day, the candle-end
of a soul. I wept then
for the spent match of my life:

at what point may a man call himself happy?

III. Catalogue of ships

She was down on all fours
me behind on top of her clutching
the rough mane of her hair
our heaving backs to the dull heat
of the burning city
same old war only game in town

groundhog day but what I missed
was the *hapax legomenon*
of the wren in the spindle-tree.
The next time we were shipping slaves
POWs from Scythia Phrygia Lydia
Syria Ilyria floggable goods

even in cloudcuckooland
exchangeable for alcohol muskets
fine-art *bògòlanfini*.. Somewhere
there's a beach of long-bones, delicate
manacled wrist-bones you could scoop up
in handfuls. *In Phylace*

*he left behind a wife to tear her cheeks
in grief* in Ghana Guinea Benin
in Congo Mozambique *las aventuras
de un marino sin escrúpulos*
but with a terrible itch for travel
and consequently I may never find now

the deepest romance the love
of my life my grandson asleep
newborn on my chest. Such a short time left
to finish the round trip, build the wharves
and warehouses, sew up the bag of winds –

And when, where, how or ever again?...

IV. Tanguedad

Yet is it not beautiful to think
how the very first of us
shouldering our grandmothers
across the break-neck olduvai boulders
rowed our kin and kine
on kontiki-rafts over unpacific oceans

as far as terra nullius
to the rough ground of no one's
land north of mount pleasant
though often forced to turn back
on account of the many *aporiai*
and the terrible *erēmia*

encountered on the gyring sea.
Steering by Carina the keel Puppis
the poop deck Pyxis the compass Vela
the sails we docked for a while
in the tall shadows of a sprawling port city
to dance in the arms

of other men.
We found our feet on the uneven floors
of tenements and bars in a trance
of intimacy, guitar and barrel organ
on the dark side of town
waiting for work, for women,

for the wind to turn.
It had been a golden age, pure sunshine,
learning the ladies' part
la Cunita then we were gone
to Monte Verde
Xihoudu Atapuerca Java

– *quién sabe cuándo te vuelva a ver?*

V. Torch

Meanwhile Helen: *'this is a handwritten letter
in the old style because I am in Thalassa
one of the dune shacks lent me
by my doctor friend. There's no electricity
– I am writing by the glow
from two kerosene lamps*

*which I have learned to feed, trim & clean.
Also a kind of miner's lantern
that you wear on your head
so it lights up in a small LED-like way
wherever you turn, like a thought
illuminating whatever it alights on.*

*The toilet is a boat-shaped outhouse.
There is no water
except from a well fifty yards away,
I haul it in gallon bottles
a hundred steps back up the dune.
It is a minimalist sublime,*

*sand, a few sturdy plants, the sea –
& the sky, hugely active
here at the edge.
Strange to swim as I did today in an ocean
where no-one can see you,
out of time.*

*I don't know
how I could have thought of finishing my story
without this immersion.
Out there alone, I swam alone,
no friends, lovers,
it felt as if I were part of the ocean…'*

Was it then she began the poem, started a war?

VI. Ora Maritima

A toddler is playing with his paper boats
in a shallow basin filled
and re-filled by his laughing mother,
to the north Thule to the south
Cinnamonifera Regio to the west
Ierne to the east Ugarit. Then a breath

of breeze silvering the surface, tippling
the boats, rivulets of liquid
slaking the dust, all the tributaries
of Scamander spattering the plain.
Baby Sikandar giggles and smacks his hands
on the water, loving the piss

and spray of it, little despot-god
of rainbows and tsunamis
– cities of ants stream out of the soil
desperate to save their treasury of eggs,
origami fleets thrown to the wind
stamped on, flattened. We scramble

ashore *qua profundum semel insinuat saxum*
Bluff Cove Ajax Bay, mariners
turned marines, that time we spent
the whole forest-fire summer in Marseille
wiped from our minds in a welter
of logistics and requisitions

helicopters lost in fog on a glacier
the injured airlifted out we could
hear them screaming the fleetship
burning and buckling for a week
this was war but we were just boys
in the long hot days on the lido –

O say was you ever in Rio Grande? O was you ever on that strand?

VII. Imagining Albion

Fell water's retching into the stone basin
a *perpetuum mobile* of rain river sea rain
around and around, the resurrection cockleshell
not due for a century or three with its end-of-the-world-
as-we-know-it, its in-the-beginning god-was-a-wording,
its gold-leafed leather-bound carolingians

and blessed beehive huts, the clear heather honey
of contemplation. Stuck in the twilight
of the old gods we repeat the actions of yesterday
and the year before, the mauve coast unravelling
in front of us as fast as our keels could have stitched it
into a story knot by knot for our grandchildren

– a white doe in the brief sea-smoke
on a headland, same dreams, nightmares,
same old odyssey-shmodyssey, a sea-dog
turned to stone on the beach. The tide going out,
the tide coming in, the tide going out,
our names worn smooth in the mirror-work

of pools, Thales-the-world-walks-on-water,
Anaximander 'n Anaximenes all hot air and playing-
misty-for-me, c'mon-light-my-fire Herakleitos
never stopping long enough to step into the same river
once. Stay calm and carry on, my matelots,
soon there'll be promenades and Salley Gardens,

ice-cream parlours, bandstands, stand-up,
in-and-out-and-shake-it-all-about
and girls, girls, girls, girls, girls!
Then far out in the bay of a kiss-me-quick evening
you'll turn back landwards to semaphore
to your sweetheart the pink-lit-neon tribute –

but will you still love me tomorrow?

VIII. Wreck

Even so this is no pilgrimage.
The eyes of the whitewashed crofts
are bordered with blue, ivy
almost covers the forgetful well.
It is a question of pride –
all heroes including Mr O

are intent on getting there sooner or later.
Constellations caught in its dark
glint their celestial plankton
em luzentes assentos, marchetados
de ouro e perlas, foxfire
bright enough to tell the flotsam by,

a pool of violets and naufrage
where centaurs and camelopards rise and set and rise again.
Into this moonless microclimate,
inferno of the drowned who will not rise,
plunge Sindbad and all the true and able seamen
embarked on the night sea-journey

the descent to where psychosis waits
with its upward-pointing mouth, stargazer,
bottom-feeder, there is no return.
We touch our collars, wear the windrose
under our skin, cross the line on hands and knees:
any other answer and the mermaid

will send this temple our ship *Sea Venture Pequod Esmeralda*
down again and again with all hands
and a cargo of scarlet
heading for Fiddler's Green
where land no longer is
nor sea nor air

– was there ever chummies now such as you and I, Jack?

IX. Shanty

Let's make a songbook of the drowned
who succumb to the uncontrollable urge
to breathe, Antinoüs
until his footing disappeared from under him
and still drowsy he went below the waves
or those who die incapable

of waving or shouting for help
in baths buckets puddles toilets
under the influence or silently
by nitrogen narcosis, laryngospasm,
self-induced hypocapnia. We lost them
to hallucinations of foureye

butterflyfish, sailfins planing
over the equator to sleep on shore.
Shelley at Livorno Hart Crane
in the Gulf of Mexico Palinurus
o nimium caelo et pelago confise sereno
l'Inconnue de la Seine –

opheliac details usually lost
in bodies taken from the water
bloated and floating
off another cape of good hope.
The drowned upon the bank are left to wonder.
But every seven years excepting Fridays

you'll be allowed ashore
to search for the most-kissed face
the kelp-haired woman
Resusci-Annie among the dune grasses
drumming her hand-on-heart music
through the short northern night

– recognise your daughter lover mother wife?

X. Trans

Or see it this way: the poet becalmed
by the sex s/he's in, hir spirit's vessel,
that satin slipper out of which the trickle
of verse spills, gendered already. Don't
you love the way Naso writes about
love, like a man but just like a woman?

At ille, but the boy, wiggling his toes
in the play of the lake-shore's ripples,
decides to strip off and dive in. He knows
what he's doing, the nymph's mad
for him, hot. So he swims to and fro
in front of her, up and down, back and forth,

butt-naked, gorgeous. She, *illa,*
watches for an hour or three. Then something
gives and she turns: octopus to ivy, ivy
to python, her undulations and suckers
gripping him every which way till –
how sweet – they become one, mix 'n match,

neither and both. It was the single trip
I was hell-bent on making, flailing across
to the other side. Lady Teiresias. Who
understands birdsong. Which could be code
for poetry. Meanwhile over in Napoli
ciao belle ragazze! Evviva il coltinello,

Porporino, Farinelli, Caffarelli! I'm starting
iam non voce virili to get my sea legs.
Sigmund says – well, you know how it goes
– but it's the price you must pay.
Like a man but just like a woman.
Sur la scène l'illusion était complète,

is it not better this way?

XI. Thule

It was much later we hung our wet shirts
over the branches of stunted trees
warming our sea-chilled flesh
in the sudden sun, watching
a hang-glider cloud, daydreaming
of Massalia its wayside shrines

and window-boxes, aromas
of *pissoirs* and beer, the whole
veranda-jacaranda makeover,
young cats stalking the clover-lawns,
uton wé hycgan hwær wé hám ágen.
lord I feel so broke up

I wanna go home *ond ðonne*
geþencan hú wé ðider cumen
the sun dripping through the leaves
and steam rising off the ship's flank,
all my iron men singing.
But we're coasting north of Orkas,

it's like a time-lapse movie
of one man's obsession – hogging trusses
cross-braced hull-beams then the slots
for one hundred and seventy-four oar-blades
that stroke the waves at six knots
non-stop for a day and a half

says Thucydides, using the old measure,
and in the tavernas
the crew could talk of nothing else.
Folk we met there spoke with a Prettanic lisp,
lived at peace, we rowed on to where
sun never rises, sea's frozen utterly over –

would I ever tell you a lie?

XII. Nostos

The wheel turns around and around,
the tide goes out. When it comes in again
I'll be a woman landlocked
as far as can be from the sea's snarl and spurn
in a four-square house with a flung-open window
whose green light ripples long fingers

through the leaves of her hair
and all the while she's lulling a wakeful child
and the moon will not remind her
of tides, she will never wish
to swim between grey seals of rock
out to the greyer waste *halos atrugetoio*

swirling with dead fish and plastic trash,
her baths will be scented with salts of rose
she will step into the silk of it
and out on to dry land
not swaying beneath her, she will not heave up
the heart and soul of her guts over the side,

she knows the words of shanties from school.
O I have sailed twenty-three centuries to become her
pacing the bedroom floor cradling
the child skin to skin
rinsing his lotus-bud head in lucid rivulets.
Her bones will root whitely in earth

earth-worms not lampreys will have her.
There she is waving the flag of her hanky
to *the Golden Hind the Argo the Mary Rose*
though I can barely see her or the child
across the silver mile of our wake. The cape
is whistling through its shark-teeth:

o did you ever see a wild goose sailin' o'er the sea?

Notes

Section I.
Kantion, Belerion, Orkas are the ancient Greek names for Kent, Cornwall and the Orkneys.

Section II.
piceum fert fumida lumen / et commixtam Volcanus ad astra favillam (Vergil, *Aeneid* IX, 75–6) = the smoking branches threw / a pitchy glow, and Vulcan hurled the cloud of ashes to heaven (Translation by A. S. Kline).

Section III.
In Phylace / he left behind a wife to tear her cheeks – from the translation of *Iliad* II by Ian Johnston (line 700).

'Los Pilotos de Altura' narra las aventuras de un marino sin escrúpulos dedicado al comercio de esclavos. – '*The Pilots of High Altitude*' follows the adventures of a sailor without scruples engaged in the slave trade (from the jacket description of the novel by the Spanish Basque author Pío Baroja, first published in 1931).

And when where, how or ever again?… – from *Anathémata,* David Jones, p. 93.

Section IV.
quién sabe cuándo te vuelva a ver? (from a tango song) = who knows when I will return to see you again?

Section V.
Edited extracts from a friend's letter, used with permission.

Section VI.
qua profundum semet insinuat saxum / Oceano ab usque (Avienus, *Ora Maritima,* 82–3) = …where a huge outcrop of rock rises all the way from deep Ocean… (own translation [of disputed text]).

Section VIII.
Em luzentes assentos, marchetados / de ouro e perlas... (From Luis de Camões, *Os Lusiadas*, Canto I) = [the gods] in shiny seats, enamelled of gold and pearls... (Translator unknown).

Section IX.
until his footing disappeared from under him / and still drowsy he went below the waves – from 'The Statue of Antinous', Sue Boyle.

o nimium caelo et pelago confise sereno, / nudus in ignota, Palinure, iacebis harena (Vergil, *Aeneid* V, 870–1) = Ah too trustful in calm skies and seas thou shalt lie, O Palinurus, naked on an alien sand! (Translation by J. W. Mackail).

The drowned upon the bank are left to wonder – translation (unpublished) by Chris Miller of a line from *Ars Aemulatoria*, Érico Nogueira.

Section X.
Alludes to Ovid's tale of Hermaphroditus (*Metamorphoses IV*) and Casanova's account of a castrato's performance (*Histoire de ma vie*, Volume V, chapter XI).

evviva il coltinello = long live the little knife.

Section XI.
Uton we hycgan hwær we ham agen / ond þonne geþencan hu we þider cumen (*The Seafarer*, 117–8) = Let us now ponder where we have a home, / and then think how we will come thither (Text and translation on Anglo-Saxons.net).

and in the taverna the crew could talk of nothing else – from John Coates' lecture 'Some engineering concepts applied to ancient Greek trireme warships', 2005.

Section XII.
halos atrugetoio (Homer, *Iliad* I, 316) = of the unploughed sea.

www.ingramcontent.com/pod-product-compliance
Lightning Source LLC
Chambersburg PA
CBHW021949040426
42448CB00008B/1309